All About Mammals

by Helen Gregory

Consultant:
Adria F. Klein, Ph.D.
California State University, San Bernardino

capstone classroom
Heinemann Raintree • Red Brick Learning
division of Capstone

Mammals are one of the six groups of animals.

All mammals have hair or fur.

Some mammals have very short hair or very little hair.

Some mammals have
a lot of hair.

Baby mammals get milk from their mothers.

Many baby mammals learn how to stay alive from their mothers.

Mice take care of their babies for just a few weeks.

Humans take care of their babies for a long time.

All mammals have backbones.

This giraffe has a very long backbone!

All mammals need
to breathe air.
Pigs breathe air.

Whales and dolphins breathe the air, too.

Mammals are warm-blooded.

The body of a mammal stays the same temperature all the time.

Mammals can live in hot or cold weather. Are you a mammal?